TABLE OF CONTENTS

Was Sandy Hook a Hoax?
Sandy Hook Hoax Allegations are Disturbing!
©Copyright 2013 by Dr Leland Benton

DISCLAIMER AND TERMS OF USE AGREEMENT:

(Please Read This Before Using This Book)

This information is for educational and informational purposes only. The content is not intended to be a substitute for any professional advice, diagnosis, or treatment.

The author and publisher of this book and the accompanying materials have used their best efforts in preparing this book.

The author and publisher make no representation or warranties with respect to the accuracy, applicability, fitness, or completeness of the contents of this book. The information contained in this book is strictly for educational purposes. Therefore, if you wish to apply ideas contained in this book, you are taking full responsibility for your actions.

The author and publisher disclaim any warranties (express or implied), merchantability, or fitness for any particular purpose. The author and publisher shall in no event be held liable to any party for any direct, indirect, punitive, special, incidental or other consequential damages arising directly or indirectly from any use of this material, which is provided "as is", and without warranties. As always, the advice of a competent legal, tax, accounting, medical or other professional should be sought where applicable.

The author and publisher do not warrant the performance, effectiveness or applicability of any sites listed or linked to in this book. All links are for information purposes only and are not warranted for content, accuracy or any other implied or explicit purpose. No part of this may be copied, or changed in any format, or used in any way other than what is outlined within this course under any circumstances. Violators will be prosecuted.

Introduction – The Best Lie Is Always Sandwiched Between Two Truths

Dr. Leland Benton is Chief Forensics Investigator for ForensicsNation.com and is a bestselling author of almost a dozen books on cyber crime. Using his investigative skills he examines the allegations that the shootings at Sandy Hook Elementary School were a hoax.

On December 14, 2012, Adam Lanza fatally shot twenty children and six adult staff members at Sandy Hook Elementary School in the village of Sandy Hook in Newtown, Connecticut.

Recent allegations and a plethora of YouTube videos have arisen that the events at Sandy Hook are all a hoax. A hoax not in the sense of whether the events took place, but more along the lines that it was a setup or staged to occur.

On the surface, this is quite disturbing to me for two reasons. If the allegations are true then we as a nation are confronting another serious problem; and if they are false, then this is a very cruel burden to place on the grieving families.

As a trained investigator, I will look dispassionately at both sides and allow my readers to decide for themselves.

I was taught that the best lie is always sandwiched between two truths. On the surface, what is to be gained if the allegations prove to be true? And conversely, what is to be gained if the allegations prove to be false? Where is the winner in all of this?

These questions and many more are presently coursing through my brain and as I begin any investigation, the questions come at me rapidly and demand answers.

Truth can be elusive, but sooner than later the truth always prevails.

Forensics is defined as the collection and preservation of evidence. I am not a law enforcement office. I catch bad guys and cyber-criminals and then call in law enforcement to make an arrest.

As Chief Forensics Investigator of ForensicsNation, I control the investigations worldwide of our over 22,000 investigators and make sure they are trained properly and adhere to the standards and guidelines published by our legal and compliance divisions.

In forensics training, a good investigator will begin to gather the facts and evidence. This is the sequence all of our investigators follow:

- Motive
- Timeline of Events
- Identity of Perpetrators
- Accomplices
- Modus operandi – techniques used to perpetrate the crime
- Gather Physical Evidence
- Identify and Interview Witnesses
- Compile & Preserve All Evidence

So let's begin with what we know.   This brief is taken from Wikipedia:

http://en.wikipedia.org/wiki/Sandy_Hook_Elementary_School_shooting

On December 14, 2012, 20-year-old Adam Lanza fatally shot twenty children and six adult staff members at Sandy Hook Elementary School in the village of Sandy Hook in Newtown, Connecticut. Before driving to the school, Lanza had shot and killed his mother, Nancy, at their Newtown home.   As first responders arrived, he committed suicide by shooting himself in the head.

The incident was the second deadliest school shooting in United States history, after the 2007 Virginia Tech massacre. It was also the second-deadliest mass murder at an American elementary school, after the 1927 Bath School bombings in Michigan.

The shooting prompted renewed debate about gun control in the United States, and a proposal for new legislation banning the sale and manufacture of certain types of semi-automatic weapons and magazines with more than ten rounds of ammunition.

Background
As of November 30, 2012, Sandy Hook Elementary School had 456 children enrolled in kindergarten through fourth grade. According to school authorities, the school's security protocol had recently been upgraded, requiring visitors to be individually admitted after visual and identification review by video monitor. The doors to the school were locked at 9:30 am each day, after morning arrivals.

Newtown is located in Fairfield County, Connecticut, about 60 miles (97 km) outside New York City. Violent crime had been rare in the town of 28,000 residents; there was only one homicide in the town in the ten years prior to the school shooting.

Shootings

Sometime before 9:30 a.m. EST on Friday, December 14, 2012, Lanza fatally shot his mother, Nancy Lanza, age 52, at their Newtown home. Investigators later found her body, clad in pajamas, in her bed with four gunshot wounds to her head. Lanza then drove to Sandy Hook Elementary School.

At about 9:35 am, using his mother's Bushmaster XM15-E2S rifle, Lanza shot his way through a locked glass door at the front of the school. He was wearing black clothing, earplugs and an olive green utility vest carrying magazines for the Bushmaster. Initial reports that he had been wearing body armor were incorrect. Some of those present heard initial shots on the school intercom system, which was being used for morning announcements.

Principal Dawn Hochsprung and school psychologist Mary Sherlach were meeting with other faculty members when they heard gunshots. Hochsprung and Sherlach immediately left the room, rushed to the source of the sounds, and encountered and confronted Lanza. He shot and killed both women.

Hochsprung may have turned on the school intercom to alert others in the building. A nine-year-old boy said he heard the shooter say: "Put your hands up!" and someone else say "Don't shoot!", people yelling and many gunshots over the intercom as he, his classmates, and teacher took refuge in a closet in the gymnasium. Diane Day, a school therapist who was at the faculty meeting, heard screaming, followed by more gunshots. Natalie Hammond, lead teacher in the meeting room, pressed her body against the door to keep it closed. Lanza shot Hammond through the door, in her leg and arm. She was later treated at Danbury Hospital. The police reported that a second adult was wounded in the attack, but that individual was not publicly identified.

In a first-grade classroom, Lauren Rousseau, a substitute teacher, was shot and killed. Most of the students in her class were killed; a six-year-old girl was the sole survivor. The girl's family pastor said that she survived the mass shooting by playing dead and remaining still until the building grew quiet, and she felt it was safe to leave. She ran from the school, and was the first child to escape the building. When she reached her mother, she said, "Mommy, I'm okay, but all my friends are dead." The child described the shooter as a very angry man.

Lanza then went to another first-grade classroom nearby. The classroom's teacher, Victoria Leigh Soto, was reported to have attempted to hide several children in a closet and cupboards. As Lanza entered her classroom, Soto reportedly told him that the children were in the auditorium. Several of the children then came out of their hiding place and tried to run for safety and were shot dead. Soto put herself between her students and the shooter, who then fatally shot her. Six surviving children from Soto's class crawled out of the cupboards after the shooting and fled the school. They and a school bus driver took refuge at a nearby home. As reported by his parents, a six-year-old boy in Soto's class fled with a group of his classmates and the children escaped through the door when Lanza shot their teacher.

Anne Marie Murphy, a teacher's aide who worked with special-needs students, shielded six-year-old Dylan Hockley with her body, trying to protect him from the bullets that killed them both. Teacher's aide Rachel D'Avino, who had been employed at the school working with a special-needs student for a little more than one week, also died trying to protect her students.

School nurse Sally Cox, 60, hid under a desk in her office and described the door opening and seeing Lanza's boots and legs facing her desk from approximately 20 feet (6.1 m) away. He remained standing for a few seconds before turning around and leaving. She and school Secretary Barbara Halstead then hid in a first-aid supply closet for up to four hours, after calling 9-1-1. Custodian Rick Thorne ran through hallways, alerting classrooms.

First grade teacher Kaitlin Roig, age 29, hid 14 students in a bathroom and barricaded the door, telling them to be completely quiet to remain safe. School library staff Yvonne Cech and Maryann Jacob first hid 18 children in a part of the library the school used for lockdown in practice drills, but on discovering that one of the doors

9

would not lock, had the children crawl into a storage room as Cech barricaded the door with a filing cabinet.

Music teacher Maryrose Kristopik, 50, barricaded her fourth-graders in a tiny supply closet during the rampage. Lanza arrived moments later, pounding and yelling "Let me in", while the students in Kristopik's class quietly hid inside.

Two third graders, chosen as classroom helpers, were walking down the hallway to the office to deliver the morning attendance sheet as the shooting began. Teacher Abbey Clements pulled both children into her classroom, where they hid.

Laura Feinstein, a reading specialist at the school, gathered two students from outside her classroom and hid with them under desks after they heard gunshots.

Feinstein called the school office and attempted to call 9-1-1 but was unable to connect because her cell phone did not have reception. She hid with the children for approximately 40 minutes, before law enforcement came to lead them out of the room.

Lanza stopped shooting between 9:46 am and 9:49 am, after firing 50 to 100 rounds. He reloaded frequently during the shooting, sometimes firing only fifteen rounds from a thirty round magazine. He shot all of his victims multiple times, and at least one victim, six-year-old Noah Pozner, 11 times. Most of the shooting took place in two first-grade classrooms near the entrance of the school, killing fourteen in one room and six in the other. The student victims were eight boys and twelve girls, between six and seven years of age, and the six adults were all women who worked at the school. Bullets were also found in at least three cars parked outside the school. After realizing that he had been spotted by a pair of police officers who had entered the building, Lanza fled from their sight and then killed himself with a gunshot to the head with a handgun.

First response
Newtown police dispatch first requested officers on the scene at 9:35 am Connecticut State Police received the first call at 9:41 am,

and with Newtown police, quickly mobilized local police dog and police tactical units, a bomb squad, and a state police helicopter.

Police locked down the school and began evacuating the survivors room-by-room, escorting groups of students and adults away from the school. They swept the school for additional shooters at least four times. No shots were fired by the authorities. According to a transcript of police radio traffic, Lanza committed suicide within fifteen minutes of the first 911 call being received.

At approximately 10:00 am, Danbury Hospital scrambled extra medical personnel in expectation of having to treat numerous victims. Three wounded patients were evacuated to the hospital, where two children were later declared dead. The other was an unidentified adult.

The New York City medical examiner dispatched a portable morgue to assist the authorities. The victims' bodies were removed from the school and formally identified during the night after the shooting. A state trooper was assigned to each victim's family to protect their privacy and provide them with information.

Investigation
A large quantity of unused ammunition was recovered inside the school, along with three semi-automatic firearms found with Lanza: a .223-caliber Bushmaster XM15-E2S rifle, a 10mm Glock handgun and a 9mm SIG Sauer P226 handgun. A 30 round magazine was recovered with the rifle. Outside the school, an Izhmash Saiga-12 combat shotgun was found in the car Lanza had driven. At home, Lanza had access to three more firearms: a .45 Henry repeating rifle, a .30 Enfield rifle, and a .22 Marlin rifle.

The weapons were legally owned by Lanza's mother, who was a gun enthusiast. Police said that Lanza used the Bushmaster rifle to kill the victims at the school. At a press conference on December 15, Dr. H. Wayne Carver II, the Chief Medical Examiner of Connecticut, was asked about the wounds, and replied "All the ones that I know of at this point were caused by the long weapon." Under

Connecticut law, the 20-year-old Lanza was old enough to carry a long gun, but too young to legally own or carry handguns.

Investigators are not believed to have found a suicide note or any messages referring to the planning of the attack. Janet Robinson, superintendent of Newtown schools, said she had not found any connection between Lanza's mother and the school, in contrast to initial media reports that stated Lanza's mother had worked there. Lanza removed the hard drive from his computer and damaged it prior to the shooting, creating a challenge for investigators to recover data. Investigators have evaluated Lanza's body, looking for evidence of drugs or medication through toxicology tests. Additionally, although unusual for an investigation of this type and unlikely to provide conclusive information, DNA testing of Lanza is being utilized.

Police also investigated whether Lanza was the person who had been in an altercation with four staff members at Sandy Hook School the day before the massacre. It was presumed that he killed two of the four staff members involved in the altercation (the principal and the psychologist) and wounded the third (the lead teacher) in the attack; the fourth staff member was not at the school that day. The state police stated that they did not know of any reports about any altercations at the school.

Police sources initially reported Lanza's sibling, Ryan Lanza, as the perpetrator. This was likely because the perpetrator was carrying his brother's identification, Ryan told *The Jersey Journal*. Lanza's brother voluntarily submitted to questioning by New Jersey police, Connecticut State Police, and the Federal Bureau of Investigation. Police said he was not considered a suspect, and he was not taken into custody. Ryan Lanza said he had not been in touch with his brother since 2010. Connecticut State Police indicated their concern about misinformation being posted on social media sites and threatened prosecution of anyone involved with such activities.

Perpetrator
Adam Peter Lanza was born on April 22, 1992, in Exeter, New Hampshire. He and his mother lived in Sandy Hook, 5 miles (8 km)

from the elementary school. He did not have a criminal record. He attended Sandy Hook Elementary School for a brief time. Afterward, he attended St. Rose of Lima Catholic School in Newtown, and then Newtown High School, where he was an honors student. Lanza subsequently was home-schooled by his mother, and earned a GED. Lanza's aunt said his mother removed him from the Newtown public school system because she was unhappy with the school district's plans for her son. He attended Western Connecticut State University in 2008 and 2009.

Adam Lanza

Students and teachers who knew him in high school described Lanza as "intelligent, but nervous and fidgety". He avoided attracting attention and was uncomfortable socializing. He is not known to have had any close friends in school.

Lanza's brother told law enforcement that Adam was believed to have a personality disorder and was "somewhat autistic". An anonymous law enforcement official and friends of Nancy Lanza reported that Adam had been diagnosed with Asperger syndrome Due to concerns that published descriptions of Lanza's autism could result in a backlash against others with the condition, autism advocates campaigned to clarify that autism is a brain-related developmental problem and not a mental illness. The predatory aggression demonstrated in the shooting is generally not seen in the autistic population.

Following her divorce from Adam's father, a corporate executive, Nancy Lanza was supported by alimony payments. A relative commented that she did not have to work because the divorce settlement had left her "very well off". There were conflicting reports on whether she had worked as a volunteer at the Sandy Hook Elementary School.

According to Nancy Lanza's sister-in-law, she was a gun enthusiast and owned at least a dozen firearms. She often took her two sons to a local shooting range.

Reactions

President Obama's remarks on the day of the shooting

President Barack Obama gave a televised address the day of the shootings, saying, "We're going to have to come together and take meaningful action to prevent more tragedies like this, regardless of the politics." Obama expressed "enormous sympathy for families that are affected". He also ordered flags to be flown at half-staff at the White House and other U.S. federal government facilities worldwide in respect of the victims. On December 16, Obama traveled to Newtown where he met with victims' families and spoke at an interfaith vigil. President Obama will honor the six slain adults posthumously with the 2012 Presidential Citizens Medal on February 15, 2013.

Flowers for the victims from people of Newtown

Connecticut Governor Dan Malloy addressed the media the evening of the shootings near a local church holding a vigil for the victims, urging the people of Connecticut to come together and help each other. Malloy said, "Evil visited this community today, and it is too early to speak of recovery, but each parent, each sibling, each member of the family has to understand that Connecticut, we are all in this together, we will do whatever we can to overcome this event, we will get through it." Hundreds of mourners, including Malloy, attended vigils in various churches in Newtown. On December 17, Malloy called for a statewide moment of silence and church bells to be tolled 26 times at 9:30 am on Friday, December 21, exactly one week after the school shooting.

U.S. Secretary of Education Arne Duncan said "... our thanks go out to every teacher, staff member, and first responder who cared for, comforted, and protected children from harm, often at risk to themselves. We will do everything in our power to assist and support the healing and recovery of Newtown."

A makeshift memorial on Berkshire Road in Sandy Hook

The day after the shootings, Lanza's father released a statement:

"Our hearts go out to the families and friends who lost loved ones and to all those who were injured. Our family is grieving along with all those who have been affected by this enormous tragedy. No words can truly express how heartbroken we are. We are in a state of disbelief and trying to find whatever answers we can. We too are asking why. We have cooperated fully with law enforcement and will continue to do so. Like so many of you, we are saddened, but struggling to make sense of what has transpired."

Leaders from many countries and organizations throughout the world also offered their condolences through the weekend after the shooting.

Minute of silence observed in the White House on December 21, 2012

In his speech at the December 16 vigil, Obama called for using "whatever power this office holds", to prevent similar tragedies in the future. Within 15 hours of the incident, 100,000 Americans signed a petition at the Obama administration's We the People petitioning website in support of a renewed national debate on gun control. President Obama later affirmed that he would make gun control a "central issue" at the start of his second term of office, in a speech on December 19. The President formed a Gun Violence Task Force to be led by Vice President Joe Biden to address the causes of gun violence in the United States. Senators Dianne Feinstein and Joe Lieberman called for an assault weapon ban, with Feinstein

16

intending to introduce a ban bill on the first day of the new Congress, while former Congresswoman Gabrielle Giffords, who was shot and injured in a 2011 shooting in Tucson, has launched Americans for Responsible Solutions to raise money for further gun control efforts in light of the Sandy Hook shooting. Fear of future restrictions on firearms led to a spike in sales of guns, ammunition, and magazines in the weeks following the shooting.

A month after the shooting, President Obama cited the incident while announcing proposals for increased gun control. His proposals included universal background checks on firearms purchases, an assault weapons ban, and limiting magazine capacity to 10 cartridges. Relatives of the victims in the shooting and survivors from other mass shootings were official guests during the announcement.

On December 21, 2012, the National Rifle Association called on the United States Congress to appropriate funds for the hiring of armed police officers in every American school to protect students. The NRA also announced the creation of a school protection program called the National School Shield Program, which would be led by former Drug Enforcement Administration (DEA) administrator and United States Congressman Asa Hutchinson.

Impact on the community
The school was closed indefinitely following the shooting, partially because it remained a crime scene. Sandy Hook students returned to school on January 3, 2013 at Chalk Hill Middle School in nearby Monroe at the town's invitation. Chalk Hill is a previously unused facility, refurbished after the shooting, with desks and equipment brought in from Sandy Hook Elementary. The Chalk Hill school has been temporarily renamed "Sandy Hook". The University of Connecticut created a scholarship for the surviving children of the shootings.

On January 31, 2013, the Newtown school board voted unanimously to ask for police officer presence in all of its elementary schools; previously other schools in the district had such protection, but Sandy Hook had not been one of those.

As I said earlier, I do not dispute that the events described above took place. There is no doubt that the events did occur as outlined above.

I will now look at some of the conspiracy theories to determine their validity.

Chapter 1 - Conspiracy Claim Draws 11-Million Views on YouTube

http://www.christianpost.com/news/sandy-hook-hoax-video-conspiracy-claim-draws-11m-views-on-youtube-video-88559/

The controversial Sandy Hook conspiracy video, claiming the incident was an elaborate hoax, is about to surpass 11 million views on YouTube. The "truther" video has gone amazingly viral and has also spawned numerous comments and rebuttal videos from other experts of the conspiracy theory world.

The Sandy Hook hoax video was originally posted onto YouTube on Jan. 7 and immediately attracted a lot of attention. The video has snowballed and gathered more and more viewers over recent days, and has increasingly caught the attention of others who regularly speak on conspiracies and their authenticities.

Despite the huge attention the video is getting, some experts have now stepped forward to rebuke the viral video as merely a marketing tool, which just "asks questions" rather than offering any clear-cut evidence of any conspiracy, according to a Huffington Post report.

(Photo: REUTERS/Michelle McLoughlin)

A young boy is comforted outside Sandy Hook Elementary School after a shooting in Newtown, Connecticut, December 14, 2012.

The controversial video has been entitled, "The Sandy Hook Shooting - Fully Exposed," and was posted on YouTube by user, "ThinkOutsideTheTV." The video lasts for more than 30 minutes and goes through various news reports from the Newtown massacre and interviews conducted in the aftermath of the Sandy Hook shootings.

At the start a disclaimer is posted stating, "This is a simple, logical video. No aliens, holograms [sic], rituals or anything like that, just facts."

Benjamin Radford, author of "Media Mythmakers" and deputy editor of the Skeptical Inquirer, has said, according to the Huff Post: "The video begins with something that really everybody can accept -- 'We are just raising questions. The whole subject is framed like, 'Don't look at us, we're not saying this crazy stuff, we're just asking questions.'"

(Photo: REUTERS/Eric Thayer)

People react during a prayer service at St. John's Episcopal church near Sandy Hook Elementary School in Sandy Hook, Connecticut December 15, 2012. Residents of the small Connecticut community of Newtown were reeling on Saturday from one of the worst mass shootings in U.S. history, as police sought answers about what drove a 20-year-old gunman to slaughter 20 children at an elementary school.

He added, "The classic conspiracy theorist sees the hidden hand in everything. Nothing is as it seems. There's something bigger that's going on. They don't know where it is, but they are willing to tantalize people and throw out any number of suggestions, which are oftentimes contradictory."

The Huff Post also spoke to David Mikkelson, founder of "Snopes.com": "In any kind of disaster or tragedy like this, if you go through things with a fine-toothed comb, you will find a number of contradictory statements. Of course most of them are cleared up within a few days of the initial reporting, but it's not something you're going to see in these [conspiracy] videos."

The video points to discrepancies in reports to do with the guns used in the shooting, with a rifle said to have been used by Adam Lanza in the school, but then later found in the car. It was reported later than there was a separate shotgun in the trunk of Lanza's car.

The hoax video also claims that some of the grieving parents are actors, and do not act appropriately following the horrific event.

The video maker also points to a number of memorial and fundraising websites for the Sandy Hook shootings set up a number of days before. However, some have suggested that search engine results do not always reflect accurately the date things first appeared on websites.

A combination of 12 handout pictures shows 12 of 20 young schoolchildren killed at Sandy Hook Elementary School in Newtown, Conn. on Friday, Dec. 14, 2012, in one of the worst mass shootings in U.S. history.

In one part of the video the commentator suggests one of the children killed in the shooting, 6 year old Emilie Parker, can be seen days later in a photo with President Barack Obama as he met their grieving family. However, others have pointed out that the lookalike is simply the girl's sister, who of course is still alive and did meet the president.

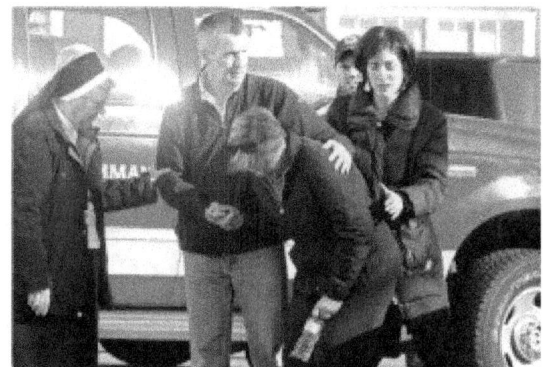

(Photo: Reuters/Michelle McLoughlin)

Relatives react outside Sandy Hook Elementary School following a shooting in Newtown, Conn., Dec. 14, 2012.

Towards the end of the video the truther commentator suggests there is an agenda why this "hoax" had been set up; to "disarm" Americans of their guns, and erode their Second Amendment rights. The video flashes up numerous articles, including one from The Christian Post, reporting on gun control proposals, and the debate surrounding new legislation on gun laws.

The video invites viewers to research the facts themselves and to look out for more postings in the future as more information emerges.

Of course, many have rebuked the video, calling it "insensitive" to the families involved in the tragedy, and especially those highlighted in the video as allegedly not grieving enough or in the appropriate way.

Here is a video of the viral Sandy Hook Shooting hoax truther posting:
http://gnli.christianpost.com/video/the-sandy-hook-shooting-fully-exposed-8209

Is any of this true? Is it possible that the Conspiracy "truthers" are correct in their allegations? Read on; it really gets interesting…

Chapter 2 – This Is The Blaze's Point-by-Point Sandy Hook Conspiracy Theory Debunk

http://www.theblaze.com/stories/2013/01/23/this-is-theblazes-point-by-point-sandy-hook-conspiracy-theory-debunk/

Was Adam Lanza *really* the only shooter at Sandy Hook Elementary School? Why are there supposed inconsistencies surrounding the weapons that were used during the attack? And are some of the parents really "crisis actors" brought in to make the situation that much more believable?

Those are only a few of the questions that have been posed by conspiracy theorists who have used the Internet to virally spread their doubt about the horrific massacre that unfolded in Connecticut on Dec. 14.

The main crux of the arguments presented in documentary-style videos is that the Sandy Hook massacre is either a government-planned hoax intended to lead the nation to overwhelmingly embrace increased gun control measures. Or, at the least, those who have put the videos out believe that essential information is being withheld from the American public surrounding multiple shooters and other game-changing elements. The motivations of those who have created these theories are difficult to pin down, as most are spouting their views anonymously.

A video documenting purported inconsistencies surrounding the tragedy that killed 20 children and six adults inside the school has gone viral, gaining more than 11 million views in just two weeks. And a follow-up "documentary" has also been released, adding further "evidence" to the claim that the event either didn't unfold at all or that it happened contrary to the media narrative that has been advanced.

To most people, the idea that any of it is true is repulsive. So we decided to visit the most popular of the theories and break them down in a point-by-point debunk.

In addition to questioning the official account of weapons used and whether or not crisis actors were employed by the government, theorists have taken aim at parental reaction to the shootings and have claimed that memorial pages for the victims were published *before* the shooting took place. And these notions only scratch the surface that is the bizarre world of Sandy Hook Trutherism.

The shadowy individual behind the first video, entitled, "The Sandy Hook Shooting – Fully Exposed" (30 minutes in length), weaves together sparse details and attempts to poke holes in the overall story. As for the first video, Snopes.com, a web site known for debunking untruthful information, dismissed it as "a mixture of misinformation, innuendo, and subjective interpretation." You can see the clip here:

http://www.youtube.com/watch?v=Wx9GxXYKx_8

The second part of the Truther initiative, titled, "Sandy Hook Fully Exposed" (19 minutes in length) tackles similar themes, builds upon the first video and attempts to defend those individuals who are questioning the details associated with the event. In addition to asking a variety of questions about family members who lost children, the videos even devote time to questioning whether "crisis actors" were brought in to speak with media in the wake of the attack. See Part II, below:

http://www.youtube.com/verify_controversy?next_url=/watch%3Fv%3DWx9GxXYKx_8%26feature%3Dplayer_embedded

"Isn't something like Sandy Hook just what the government needs to start disarming the public so they don't have to worry about people being a threat to them anymore?,' text embedded in the video reads.

TheBlaze has decided to go through both videos to provide you with a recap of the major points that Truthers are raising. In addition to presenting the arguments that those perpetuating an alleged hoax are positing, you'll see reasonable explanations that essentially debunk their claims and questions. In any crime scene – especially one as traumatic and dramatic as what unfolded at Sandy Hook – information flows quickly and it isn't uncommon for incorrect details to make their way into media. This, as you will see, is the case when it comes to numerous elements surrounding this tragic shooting.

THE MAN IN THE WOODS & ADDITIONAL SHOOTERS

Sandy Hook Truthers have spent a great deal of time and energy reporting about a man who was allegedly chased in the woods nearby the school; the individual was subsequently apprehended and the entire spectacle is captured on video — footage that is now being used to advance the idea that there was another shooter. The first "expose" shows media interviews with witnesses who claim to have seen this individual in handcuffs following the incident. If it is true that there was more than one shooter, this would obviously turn on its head everything that has been said about a lone murderer (i.e. Lanza).

The man in the woods, though, isn't the only theory about additional shooters floating around. Additionally, others claim that there were two men who fled the scene in a van. Initial media reports did say that there may have been more than one shooter involved, but as the details came in and the events were clarified, Lanza was the only gunman named and the evidence cleared every other initial suspect.

While conspiracy theorists continue to question where these additional suspects are and why the media has allegedly failed to report about them, there are some pretty convincing counter arguments and debunks surrounding this matter.

27

Heavily armed Connecticut State troopers are on the scene at the Sandy Hook School following a shooting at the school, Friday, Dec. 14, 2012 in Newtown, Conn. A man opened fire inside the Connecticut elementary school where his mother worked Friday, killing 26 people, including 18 children, and forcing students to cower in classrooms and then flee with the help of teachers and police. (AP Photo/The Journal News, Frank Becerra Jr.) MANDATORY CREDIT, NYC OUT, NO SALES, TV OUT, NEWSDAY OUT; MAGS OUT Photo: Frank Becerra Jr., AP

The Newtown Bee, a local outlet, reported that a law enforcement official told them that the man seen in the woods had a gun and was nearby the school. He was apparently an off-duty tactical squad police officer from a nearby area. Also, Chris Manfredonia, the father of a 6-year-old student at the school, was handcuffed briefly by police after he ran around the school in an effort to find his daughter. And another unidentified man was briefly detained, but later released when he was found to be an innocent bystander, Snopes.com claims.

http://www.snopes.com/politics/guns/newtown.asp

Those being interviewed by media likely saw one of these individuals, leading Truthers to suspect something sinister. Lt. Paul Vance, a media relations representative with the State of Connecticut, dismissed the notion that there were other shooters, while also highlighting and confirming the fact that authorities did end up detaining and quickly releasing other individuals.

"Were there other people detained?" Vance rhetorically asked. "The answer is yes. In the height of the battle, until you've determined who, what, when, where and why of everyone in existence…that's not unusual."

THE WEAPONS USED INSIDE THE SCHOOL & THE VICTIMS' BODIES

Another point of contention that Truthers seem to be focusing upon is the weapons that Lanza used in committing his crime. In the first video, the narrator claims that, according to media, three guns were found at the scene (two handguns and one assault rifle). Four handguns were also allegedly found inside the school. The inconsistency here comes from the Dr. H. Wayne Carver II, the chief medical examiner, who said following the incident that the assault rifle appeared to be responsible for the children's deaths.

Here's why Truthers are jumping all over the claims surrounding the assault rifle. The first video alleging a hoax claims that this particular weapon was later recovered from the trunk of the car that Lanza was driving. If this is the case, then critics are questioning how Carver's claims could be possible. The shooter clearly couldn't have used the assault rifle to commit his crimes if the weapon was in the trunk of the car the entire time.

In this photo illustration a Rock River Arms AR-15 rifle is seen on December 18, 2012 in Miami, Florida. Credit: Getty Images

But there's an understandable answer here as well. A few days after the attack, clarity surrounding the guns finally emerged. Lanza left a shotgun in the car, but he had three other weapons that were brought into the school – a Bushmaster AR-15 rifle, a Glock 10 mm and a Sig Sauer 9 mm (the latter two are handguns). The fourth weapon – the shotgun – was left in the vehicle's trunk. Carver was correct in making his claim that it was the AR-15 that was responsible for the children's deaths – a firearm that was not in the trunk as the first video indicates (CNN actually has a great primer on the weapons that expounds upon this in detail).

While we're on the subject of Carver, it's important to dispel another rumor – that the parents never saw their children's bodies. While they did not identify the bodies in their entirety, pictures of the kids' faces were provided to the families. This wasn't done to be sinister or to hide details; quite the contrary, the doctor was trying to spare the families the pain of seeing the horrific injuries the children sustained, so photos of their faces were used instead.

SCHOOL NURSE'S ALLEGED CLAIMS ABOUT THE KILLER'S MOTHER

Andrea McCarren, a reporter for WUSA, reported in the wake of the killings about a conversation she had with Sally Cox, the Sandy Hook school nurse. Cox, who McCarren described as "fairly traumatized," apparently told the reporter that she knew the killer's mother, a kindergarten teacher at the school. Initially, media reported that Lanza may have been the son of a teacher, but this was soon dispelled.

Truthers are questioning this story, though, obviously wondering how McCarren was given information about the killer and his mother that ended up being entirely untrue (they argue that the school nurse should have had the information correct and that her mention of a teacher at Sandy Hook is curious, especially considering the details we now know).

During McCarren's report, the journalist also said that the nurse expounded, claiming that Cox said that the kindergarten teacher was kind and exactly the person one would want his or her children to spend time with. Snopes notes that the USA Today also "mistakenly reported…that Nancy Lanza" was a teacher at the school. Perhaps this report and McCarren's were based on the same misinformation.

http://www.snopes.com/politics/guns/newtown.asp

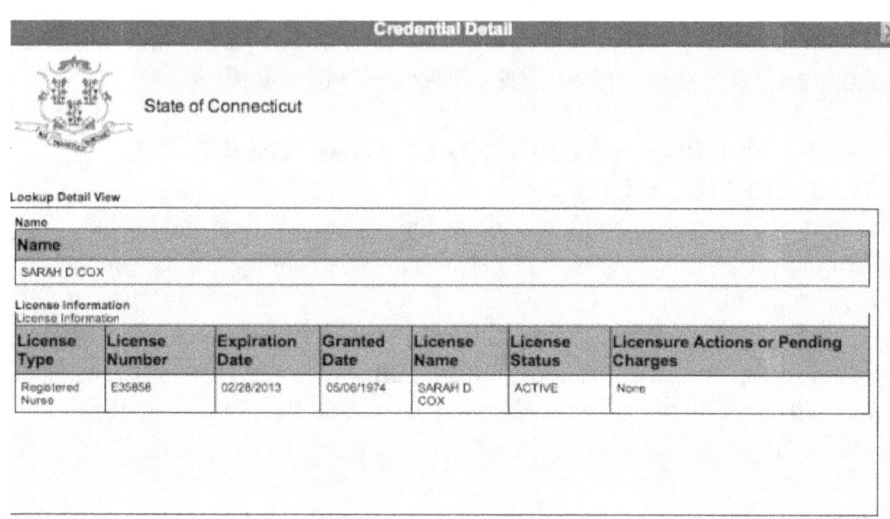

State of Connecticut

Lookup Detail View

Name

Name
SARAH D COX

License Information

License Information

License Type	License Number	Expiration Date	Granted Date	License Name	License Status	Licensure Actions or Pending Charges
Registered Nurse	E35858	02/28/2013	05/06/1974	SARAH D. COX	ACTIVE	None

1/22/2013 7:21:23 PM

Sally Cox's credentials in the State of Connecticut (Photo Credit: CT.gov)

Some have also claimed that Cox is also not a registered nurse, but her real name is Sarah and a search of that name does, indeed, yield results that show that the woman is a registered nurse in the state's registration system. Since "Sally" isn't her birth name, it's obvious that a license attacked to that name isn't available in the Connecticut database (see above).

http://www.snopes.com/politics/guns/newtown.asp

ROBBIE/EMILIE PARKER & LYNN/GRACE MCDONNELL

Emilie Parker, one of the 20 children killed at Sandy Hook, is a central character in Truthers' questioning, as they throw a number of theories about her very person and her family's reaction to her death into the mix. In addition to claiming that the young girl was Photoshopped into at least one family image, those questioning official accounts claim that her father, Robbie Parker, can be seen getting "into character" before a press conference — something they dismiss as proof that he may, indeed, be acting or playing the role of a grieving father.

This latter accusation relies upon footage of Robbie purportedly laughing before a press conference. In the clip, he can be seen smiling, taking a moment to compose himself and then allowing emotion to overtake him. "How many parents are laughing and joking a day after their first child has been shot," a text message reads across the screen in the first hoax video. Later, the words, "I smell B.S.," are added to describe the father's reaction.

The video also claims that Parker wasn't in her class photos and that she appears in images with President Barack Obama following the shooting (something that obviously wouldn't be possible had she been killed during the incident). But the below video explains that the little girl shown in the image is one of Emilie's sisters, not the young girl who perished just days before.

At least one other parent was targeted for the same reason – for appearing too chipper in the wake of losing a daughter in the horrific incident. Footage of Lynn McDonnell, mother of a child named Grace, came under scrutiny after the parent spoke with CNN's Anderson Cooper about her immense loss. While remembering her young child, she expressed facial expressions of joy. However, considering the content of her commentary (she was remembering her young child) it seemed entirely appropriate (in fact, TheBlaze covered the inspirational interview when it aired in December).

http://www.theblaze.com/stories/2012/12/24/mom-of-sandy-hook-child-victim-shares-daughters-message-from-beyond-the-grave-in-incredibly-moving-cnn-interview/

CHILD SECURITY EVENT PLANNED FOR DEC. 14
Those embracing the notion that Sandy Hook was a hoax also question an event that was put on by the Division of Emergency Management and Homeland Security (this department falls under the state's Division of Emergency Services and Public Protection). This particular event was purportedly planned before the shooting and aimed at helping explore strategies for protecting kids in the result of emergency situations like what happened that same day at Sandy Hook.

33

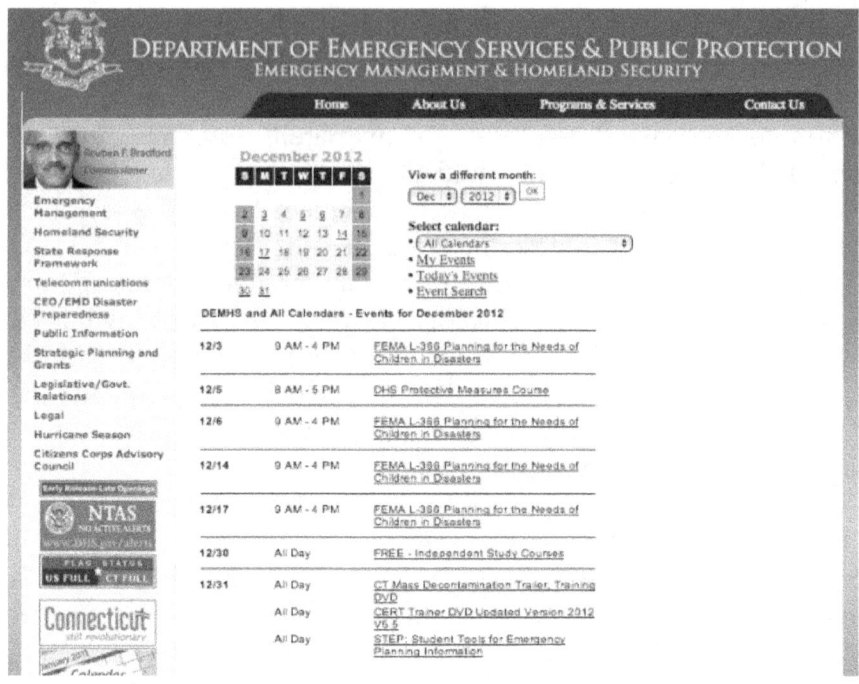

A list of classes that occurred before the training that has come under scrutiny (Photo Credit: CT.gov)

This event did occur, but it isn't as surprising as some might assume. On the surface, it may seem odd that the FEMA class, called "Planning for the Needs of Children in Disasters," was offered on the same day that Sandy Hook unfolded. But this course was also offered six additional times in the state of Connecticut during November and December. It wasn't a rare occurrence only planned on the day of the shooting; it was an event that had been repeatedly held within the state's boundaries during recent days and weeks.

MEMORIAL PAGES & ASSOCIATED INTERNET TIMESTAMPS

The Truthers are particularly fired up about various memorial pages and social media initiatives that they claim were created days before Lanza's crimes at the elementary school. In addition to teacher Victoria Soto's Facebook memorial page, which they claim was created on Dec. 10, four days before the shooting, the individuals behind the video and movement also point to a GoFundMe initiative, among others, as also having timestamps that precede the event.

Inquisitr explained how the Internet, despite being quite advanced, still has its hiccups. Here's a brief recap that explains some of the reasons behind date stamps seeming incorrect on various posts and web sites:

http://www.inquisitr.com/484738/sandy-hook-hoax-were-websites-and-facebook-groups-published-before-the-massacre/

To understand the Sandy Hook websites that seem to have been published early, you must first understand the way the internet reconciles dates as well as how Google crawls them. If a page is repurposed to host other information than it originally displayed, it may show up as having been "published" earlier.

Further, servers and sites often have incorrect dates. Having used a number of WordPress panels in my career, it is a job to keep track of where dates and times are set in order to avoid publishing in the past when scheduling a post, something that could be at play and an easily explainable factor not often acknowledged by Sandy Hook truthers.

And given the fact material can run afoul on an individual computer, a site's panel and then a search engine, sites like the United Way's Sandy Hook page could easily register as a prior date on Google.

When it comes to Google results – another target the Truthers point to – the Internet giant isn't always correct. Sometimes, search results have the incorrect dates associated with them, clearly a factor that is overlooked in the conspiracy theory videos. As for the web sites that seem to have an earlier date stamp, another theory is that certain donation and Facebook pages that were created for other reasons were edited and amended to assist with Sandy Hook efforts following the shooting. While they retained their earlier creation date, their intended purposes changed.

TheBlaze spoke with Justin Basch, CEO of Basch Solutions, a website production company. The tech expert dismissed conspiracy theorists' claims, calling them "nonsense." He explained the many ways that dates can be manipulated in WordPress (the platform running at least one of the web sites at the center of the debate).

"It's very, very easy to manipulate a date that content was published — whether it's through text, whether it's through date manipulation, etc.," Basch explained.

THE SYMPATHETIC AND HELPFUL NEIGHBOR: GENE ROSEN

Then there's Gene Rosen, the neighbor who lives nearby Sandy Hook. He began appearing in media immediately following the shooting, telling of his involvement in housing six children who had escaped the school that fateful morning. Rosen has been interviewed numerous times by the mainstream media and he has explained how he entertained the children inside of his home after they fled the school in terror.

The Truthers, though, claim that Rosen's story has some troubling inconsistencies. Among them, they charge that he is a member of the Screen Actors Guild (SAG), a professional union of acting professionals (thus, advancing the theory that he might be a crisis actor). They also claim that Rosen's story about discovering the children in his driveway changed and evolved during various appearances. While in some interviews he described the six kids sitting with a female bus driver, in at least one other account, he described a male adult talking harshly to the children, the video proclaims.

Additionally, Rosen, a retired psychologist, told reporters that the children told him their teacher, Ms. Soto, was dead. Initially, some media reported that only one child escaped the classroom where the majority of the kids perished, but this ended up not being the case (others seemingly escaped as well). Rosen also said in one interview that he saw the list of victims not long after the shooting, but conspiracy theorists claim this isn't possible, as it wasn't released until after the time he claims to have seen it.

A list of casualties, though, was released the day after the shooting and, as Snopes documents; the Gene Rosen who is a member of SAG is a different individual – one who has never lived in Connecticut. The retired psychologist at the center of this particular case has always lived in the state (while both are in their 60s, the actor is 62 and the Newtown resident is 69).

LANZA'S VEHICLE ON THE DAY OF THE SHOOTING
In the second video, which spent some time defending Truthers against attacks, a bizarre claim is made about the vehicle that Lanza drove to Sandy Hook on Dec. 14. While it has been widely reported that the car belonged to his mother, whom he also shot dead before heading to the school that morning, hoax theorists believe that the car is registered to a man named Chris Rodia.

While it may be tempting for those looking for holes in the story to wonder if Rodia was complicit in helping Lanza with the attack, Snopes.com debunks this, claiming that Rodia was pulled over at a traffic stop and, thus, ended up being named on a police scanner. Salon recaps how this particular element of the story was debunked:

http://www.salon.com/2013/01/18/your_comprehensive_answer_to_every_sandy_hook_conspiracy_theory/

This one was debunked by the theorists themselves just a few days after the shooting. Blogger Joe Quinn obtained the police audio, which definitively debunking the myth. (Rodia appeared on the scanner because he was getting pulled over in a traffic stop miles away, but his license plate doesn't match Lanza's car). "This was a huge blow, because lots of people were making big leaps on this … but we now have to look elsewhere," another amateur investigator said on YouTube.

To clarify: Rodia is not a suspect and he did not own the car that Lanza drove to the school, as the video seems to allege. Rodia was also not at the school at the time of the shooting. Snopes claims that "he was driving a different vehicle in another town at the time."

CRISIS ACTORS DEPICTED IN MEDIA

Truthers' have gone out of their way (there's even a disclaimer at the start of the first video) to claim that they are not trying to dismiss the event as though it never happened. Instead, they say that they are merely asking pertinent questions and, in a sense, exercising their civic duty as caring and in-tune Americans (a tactic likely being used to separate themselves from the criticism being thrown their way). Among those curiosities, a consistent theme emerges: The idea that crisis actors were used.

We already covered Rosen and the theory that he is one of these individuals. But there are others who are being dubbed potential crisis actors. One couple in particularly has come under scrutiny. CNN interviewed Nick and Laura Phelps, parents of two children at Sandy Hook Elementary School. In the exchange, Nick becomes emotional while describing the principal at the school as "a very special person." It's clear that the family was impacted by what unfolded.

But Truthers question the motivations, sincerity and identity of Nick and Laura, claiming that they may actually be Richard and Jennifer Sexton, two actors from Florida. This bizarre claim — that the couple was brought in to merely depict parents who have children at Sandy Hook Elementary, is one of the more curious ones being floated. The evidence being posited?

The hoax video shows images from an alleged Picasa account belonging to Richard and Jennifer (the actors). Those who believe that something isn't quite right about Sandy Hook claim that the photo album was deleted after it gained attention. In addition, Truthers are using a clip showing Laura (or Jennifer) giving what appears to be an audition or performance.

But Snopes claims that the husband and wife duos merely resemble one another and that they are not, in fact, the same individuals. While the videos seem to indicate that there may be a connection between the Crisis Actors company – a group that provides actors to simulate traumatic and disastrous events, there is no connection between the actors provided by the group and the individuals shown in media interviews. Plus, a simple web search shows that the family does, indeed, live near the school.

Crisis Actors (the company) also makes it clear that its performers do not engage in real-life events. While the video alleges connections between the Sandy Hook families and these individuals, no such connections exist. In fact, the company has gone out of its way to dispel such rumors.

http://crisisactors.org/

UNDERSTANDING THE VIDEOS AND THEIR CREATOR
While the conspiracy-laden clips have intrigued some, others find themselves completely horrified, sickened and offended by their contents — especially considering the pain that the families of Sandy Hook victims have already endured. Following the publication of the first video, reaction and media coverage was swift. As noted, the creator of the videos made it a point to vehemently defend himself against critics.

"This video was made to clear up confusion and shed light on new information. Apologies to anyone offended by the past videos," a caveat at the beginning of the second clip reads. "[W]e hope this one is easier to digest. Would you rather be hurt temporarily by the truth, or comforted forever by lies?"

Later, the anonymous individual behind the clips claims that it is unfair for critics to label him and others supporting his ideas as "Truthers" – or even "conspiracy theorists." Such labels, text embedded in the video reads, imply that those questioning the event are "over the top, crazy, and against everyone else."

"These are millions of everyday people that deserve answers to their questions," the text continues. "And it seems by labeling them like that, it's easier to dismiss them and not have to look at the facts."

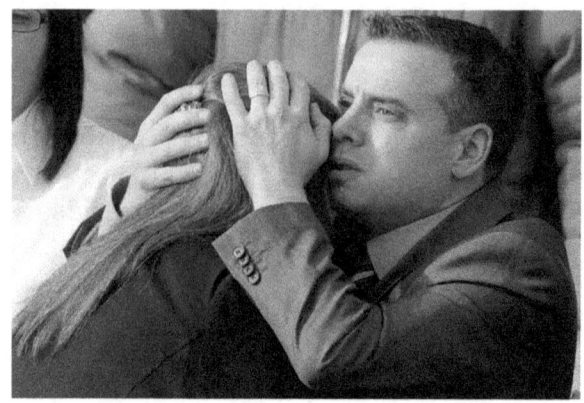

Mourners embrace following funeral services for Connecticut elementary shooting victim Emilie Parker, Saturday, Dec. 22, 2012, at The Church of Jesus Christ of Latter-day Saints, in Ogden, Utah. Emilie, 6, whose family has Ogden roots, was one of 20 children and six adult victims killed in a Dec. 14 mass shooting at Sandy Hook Elementary in Newtown, Conn. Credit: AP

However, those looking to debunk the Sandy Hook debunkers would dismiss these views as fringe. Even the person who created, "The Sandy Hook Shooting – Fully Exposed" and its companion video was surprised by its viral nature. In an interview with Gawker before the video released, he seemed surprised by its viral nature, telling the outlet that he would have "spent more time on it" if he knew it would be so popular. TheBlaze reached out to him to get further comment, but we did not receive a response.

http://gawker.com/5976204/behind-the-sandy-hook-truther-conspiracy-video-that-five-million-people-have-watched-in-one-week?tag=conspiracies

"[I]t all started when me and my friends used to research 9/11 in high school," said the source, who refused to identify himself to Gawker. "That's what really got me started when it came to researching government cover ups...Once I learned about all the false flag attacks in history that have been proven to be true, I knew it was only a matter of time before another came a long."

Apparently, in the mind of the individual behind the videos (which were published on a YouTube channel under the account ThinkOutsideTheTV), Sandy Hook was next in this purported line of government cover-ups. The individual went on to tell the outlet that he felt as though the event was "too perfect" and that the people and the town involved had an "artificial vibe about them."

OTHER THEORIES

Since Sandy Hook unfolded, other conspiracy theories have emerged, although the aforementioned YouTube clips have become the most pervasive and widespread. TheBlaze already told you about James Tracy, a communications professor at Florida Atlantic University (FAU), and his controversial comments about the Sandy Hook massacre.

http://www.theblaze.com/stories/2013/01/08/two-university-professors-wild-sandy-hook-conspiracy-theories/

Tracy, too, appeared on radio interviews, where he advanced the crisis actor angle, claiming that the Obama administration might have deployed these individuals to stage the attack in an effort to further crack down on guns. On his personal blog, he cited InfoWars.com as well. Later, he clarified his comments, claiming that while "one is left with the impression that a real tragedy took place," images and information have been withheld from the public.

The entire ordeal, which captured national attention and was covered by TheBlaze earlier this month, led FAU to separate itself from Tracy's comments. Lisa Metcalf, director of media relations, said, "James Tracy does not speak for the university."

http://www.theblaze.com/stories/2013/01/08/two-university-professors-wild-sandy-hook-conspiracy-theories/

In the same Blaze report, Jason Howerton covered Dr. James H. Fetzer, a professor emeritus at the University of Minnesota Duluth (UMD). In an op-ed published in an Iranian (state-owned, of course) outlet, he charged that, perhaps, the Mossad (Israeli security forces) were responsible for the attack.

"The killing of children is a signature of terror ops conducted by agents of Israel," he wrote. "[W]ho better to slaughter American children than Israelis, who deliberately murder Palestinian children?"

Parents leave a staging area after being reunited with their children following a shooting at the Sandy Hook Elementary School in Newtown, Conn., about 60 miles (96 kilometers) northeast of New York City, Friday, Dec. 14, 2012. An official with knowledge of Friday's shooting said 27 people were dead, including 18 children. It was the worst school shooting in the country's history. (AP Photo/Jessica Hill)

These, of course, of just two of the numerous alternative conspiracy theories being floated. There are plenty of other ideas that have circulated since Dec. 14. However, the growth in popularity of the latest videos creates some serious questions that deserve to be answered in order to properly educate readership.

At least one father of a first-grader at Sandy Hook took the issue to heart, showcasing his frustration in an on-air phone call that was placed to radio host Glenn Beck. The father, named "Pete," expressed his dismay at the conspiracy theories, calling Trutherism an "unimaginable way to even look at a tragedy or horrific event."

http://www.theblaze.com/stories/2013/01/16/dad-of-sandy-hook-first-grader-thoroughly-debunks-conspiracy-theory-that-the-shooting-never-happened-i-was-there/

"I was there. I've been to the funerals," he told Beck. "I know the families very closely. I know a lot of those children. It happened. It really happened."
But if thats not convincing enough, consider BuzzFeed's logic: "The evidence on which these budding theories are based is, even by the standards of fringe conspiracy theory, remarkably thin, and demand massive collusion between hundreds of private citizens, the federal government, local authorities, and the news media."

While the viral nature of the videos has begun to simmer, the mainstream media has not provided a level of coverage that would disseminate the truth fervently enough to dispel the rumors. Setting the record straight and showcasing the truth, though, is essential.

Chapter 3 – Analyzing the Conspiracy Theories

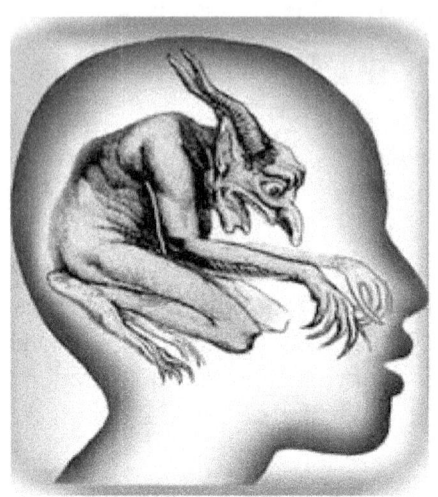

End the Sandy Hook shooting conspiracy theories
February 12, 2013

http://articles.mcall.com/2013-02-12/opinion/mc-government-conspiracies-barron-20130212_1_conspiracy-theories-sandy-hook-gun-control-laws

Ever since the Sept. 11 attack in New York City by al-Qaida, people have been coming up with conspiracies that our government is against our country. The most recent tragedy happened in Connecticut where 20 students, ages 6 and 7, were shot in their elementary school. YouTube has more than 10 videos of different people trying to convince us that our government set up the shooting so that gun control laws can be approved.

The conspiracies need to stop. Our government would not want to kill the amount of people that these videos are saying. Most of the members of the government have kids, so why would they want to kill others when they know what is would feel like to lose a kid? These conspiracies about our government going against our country after every attack that we have must come to an end.

*****

In the article above, The Morning Call newspaper made a plea for the conspiracy theories to come to an end. It seems that every national tragedy such as Sandy hook inspires a new set of "truthers" to step forward and offer forth videos and blog posts touting some of the most incredible conspiracy theories imaginable.

As a forensic investigator and behavioral scientist, I have the best of both worlds. As a behavioral scientist I can profile perpetrators, which assists in finding and prosecuting numerous cyber-criminals.

In analyzing the various conspiracy theories, a certain pattern develops quite quickly. A vehement hatred of government and wariness over anything that government says and does is the central impetus behind most conspiracy theories.

Hard economic times are causing people to do things they know they shouldn't do. In catching bad guys recently, a good many that we have caught have no previous criminal records.

We are now in tax season and the identity thieves are fast at work stealing identities and filing false tax claims. Last year, this cost the IRS over $6-billion in fraudulent claims. This year we are ready for them and we are nabbing them to the tune of 30-40 per day.

Also, during tax season we see a resurgence of the conspiracy theorists claim that the federal and state income taxes are illegal. These theorists are referred to as "straw man" adherents and purport each citizen to be a "sovereign entity" exempt from paying income tax. It doesn't matter that a good number of these people have been charged and successfully prosecuted for tax evasion and tax fraud; they still clamor every tax season that the government has no legal right to tax our income.

My point is this: conspiracy theories and cyber-crime is not going to go away; in fact it is only going to get worse. Anything that offers big financial reward and a chance to get away with it will draw the cyber-criminals in like moths to a flame. But by so doing this, we look for patterns of operations and techniques, which assists us in identifying and nabbing these perpetrators.

Now back to the conspiracy theories...

It is easy to understand cyber-criminals intent and reward for perpetrating their crimes – financial reward is enough for them. But what about conspiracy theorists? What do they gain from all of this? It certainly isn't financial reward. So, what actually compels them to put forth these conspiracy theories and invest the literally gobs of time and resources doing it? This is defined in the Introduction of this book as "motive". So what is their motive?

I am going to have to rely on behavioral science to answer the question. The answer falls along the following lines:

- Scarcity Thought
- Fear of Government
- The Blame Game

In **scarcity thought**, people believe that everybody is getting what really belongs to them. Advertisers and retailers use this to tout consumers into buying stuff they really don't need. Keeping up with the Joneses can be costly!!

In the case of conspiracy using scarcity thought, people believe that the government is keeping their good from them enjoying their prosperity. Government is taxing their income and taxes in general erode their ability to purchase goods and services.

This scarcity thought stems from an inherent **fear of the government** and who can blame people nowadays? The recent debates over taxing the rich and increasing taxes in general are fueling this fear of government. In California alone, I read that the combined effective income tax rate of both state and federal income tax is now a whopping 51%. WOW! Is it any wonder that people and businesses alike are fleeing California in droves?

But the biggest reason of them all is **the blame game**. It is built into our respective psyches that we are never at fault nor should we stand accountable for our actions. As I have said in my previous books, blame is a useless concept and we buy into the devil's lie by believing we are never wrong.

BUT WE ARE ACCOUNTABLE FOR OUR ACTIONS! The government will fine you or prosecute you if you fail to pay your income tax. If you go online and slander an individual, you can be held accountable in a court of law.

As this pertains to conspiracy theorists, they receive no financial reward so they falsely believe that no one will prosecute them for putting forth really stupid theories; especially theories that slander an individual. Remember, a person is innocent until proven guilty in a court of law but this doesn't stop the government nor conspiracy theorists of slamming an alleged perpetrator before the "perp" has had his/her day in court.

Whenever you see someone put forth a conspiracy theory that revolves around some national or international event, always look for the motive behind this theory. It will usually fall with the three categories cited above.

Chapter 4 – If Conspiracy Theories Are Mostly False Then Why Does The General Public So Readily Embrace Them?

CONSPIRACY THEORIES REPRESENT A KNOWN GLITCH IN HUMAN REASONING. THE THEORIES ARE OF COURSE OCCASIONALLY TRUE, BUT THEIR TRUTH IS COMPLETELY UNCORRELATED WITH THE BELIEVER'S CERTAINTY. FOR SOME REASON, SOMETIMES WHEN PEOPLE THINK THEY'VE UNCOVERED A LIE, THEY RAISE CONFIRMATION BIAS TO AN ART FORM. THEY CUT CONTEXT AWAY FROM FACTS AND ARGUMENTS AND ASSEMBLE THEM INTO REASSURING LITANIES. AND OVER AND OVER I'VE ARGUED HELPLESSLY WITH SMART PEOPLE CONSUMED BY THEORIES THEY WERE SURE WERE IRREFUTABLE, THEORIES THAT IN THE END PROVED COMPLETE FICTIONS.

YOUNG-EARTH CREATIONISTS, THE MOON LANDING PEOPLE, THE PERPETUAL MOTION SUBCULTURE – CAN'T YOU SEE YOU'RE FALLING INTO THE SAME PATTERN?

Boy, if I only had a penny for every time I am asked this question, "If Conspiracy Theories Are Mostly False Then Why Does The General Public So Readily Embrace Them?" I would be a bizzilionaire!

Read the printed words in the pic above because if nails this topic right on the head.

One of the most difficult things to do as a counselor and doctor is debate the lunacy of some people's belief systems especially when it comes to conspiracy theories. This is the operative quote from above, "They cut context away from facts and arguments and assemble them into reassuring litanies."

In other words, they believe they are right and no amount of convincing will change their mind. This is a very dangerous thought pattern, people because in many cases these very same conspiracy theorists do an incredible amount of damage like the perpetrator of each crime does but not in a violent manner. Is there a difference to killing someone physically or killing them in the media? In law, yes but in real life you need to answer the question for yourself.

History has proven that closed minds and closed thinking result in confusion and chaos and even as the alarm bells sound, people tend to ignore them, which leads to their demise.

The rise of Nazi Germany and its final solution "Endlosung" had numerous warnings of Hitler being a wolf in sheep's clothing but all of it was ignored. A good many Jews heard the warning and fled but many stayed behind and died in concentration camps.

Allied governments could see that war was coming but were afraid of their citizen's reaction, especially after the suffering that had occurred during World War I that was still fresh in people's minds.

This past year, we have witnessed "Arab Spring" as people from countries ruled by dictators have flung off their oppressing yokes in favor of new regimes. But in many cases – Egypt, Tunisia and Libya – the new regimes are just as bad as or worse than their predecessor governments.

Do you really believe that the governments of Egypt, Tunisia, and Libya really care about their citizens or do you believe they only care about their own agendas? Think about Iran, North Korea, and other dictator controlled countries. Do they really care about the well-being and prosperity of their citizens?

In the case of North Korea, they are stuck with their idiot dictator but the people of Iran voted in their Islamic government. The Arab Spring countries voted in their current regimes too and are now paying the price as the truth comes to light and the regimes finally reveal their evil intent.

Closer to home, the media makes statement such as the "public has the right to know," but the responsibility of the media to report the facts means little since they all only report what they deem necessary to promote their line of thought and beliefs. For example, The New

York Times is so slanted toward the democratic lines of thinking that any republican response is treated as an assault on their reporting.

Truth means NOTHING! Perception is everything and all forms of the media report in order to promote their perceptions. They hide behind sound bites and the general public's naivety.

It is important that you understand the subconscious mind's ability to perceive the reality that the conscious mind sees. They are rarely one in the same and perception rules over reality. The really smart operators know this and so do the conspiracy theorists. Their goal is to twist the facts and force a perception on your mind. My most favorite saying is "Lies are often sandwiched between two truths" to give them credibility and slant your thinking in favor of what they want you to believe.

Chapter 5 – Summary and Conclusions

Let's sum up what you already have learned. In investigating anything, all investigators rely on the outline below to systematically investigate any crime.

- Motive
- Timeline of Events
- Identity of Perpetrators
- Accomplices
- Modus operandi – techniques used to perpetrate the crime
- Gather Physical Evidence
- Identify and Interview Witnesses
- Compile & Preserve All Evidence

In the case of Sandy Hook, **motive** is still obscure since Adam Lanza did not leave a suicide note and destroyed the hard drive on his computer prior to committing his crime. Criminal psychologists as well as behavioral scientists are piecing together Lanza's life from "womb to tomb" to discover what could have caused this young man to snap. His family members are cooperating with law enforcement and the mental health practitioners to determine the cause of this behavior.

In this book's introduction I outlined the **timeline of events** from beginning to end. This leaves no doubt that Sandy Hook really occurred and that the theorists saying it was a staged event are completely off base.

The **identity of the perpetrator(s)** is a known fact. Adam Lanza acted alone and did not receive assistance of any kind from any individual or any entity. There were no **accomplices**.

The **modus operandi** is also known from the weapons that were used, how Lanza received access to these weapons, where they were purchased, etc. All **physical evidence** has been **gathered and preserved** and is presently being analyzed.
All **witnesses** as well as the grieving families have been interviewed extensively. There is little unknown about the events as they occurred as well as subsequent events too.

In summary, Sandy Hook has been handled properly as a crime scene and all evidence is now collected and preserved. There is virtually no doubt that Sandy Hook did occur and there has been no proof of any kind that Sandy Hook was a staged event in order to promote the gun control agenda or any other agenda.

It is true that government, media and individuals alike have used Sandy hook to promote a gun control agenda but this does not mean they went to such lengths as to stage Sandy hook and the resulting carnage.

The facts speak for themselves. In systematic science – as in forensic science – a theory is proposed and if the theory cannot be disproven then it becomes a law of science.

In the case of the numerous Sandy Hook conspiracies, all have been disproven since the facts they cite did not take place and hence, all of the conspiracy theories purported are false,

I Have a Special Gift for My Readers

I appreciate my readers for without them I am just another author attempting to make a difference.

My readers and I have in common a passion for the written word as well as the desire to learn and grow from books.

My special offer to you is a massive ebook library that I have compiled over the years. It contains hundreds of fiction and non-fiction ebooks in Adobe Acrobat PDF format as well as the Greek classics and old literary classics too.

In fact, this library is so massive to completely download the entire library will require over 5 GBs open on your desktop.

Use the link below and scan all of the ebooks in the library. You can select the ebooks you want individually or download the entire library.

The link below does not expire after a given time period so you are free to return for more books rather than clog your desktop. And feel free to give the link to your friends who enjoy reading too.

I thank you for reading my book and hope if you are pleased that you will leave me an honest review so that I can improve my work and or write books that appeal to your interests.

Okay, here is the link…

http://tinyurl.com/special-readers-promo

PS: If you wish to reach me personally for any reason you may simply write to mailto:support@epubwealth.com.

I answer all of my emails so rest assured I will respond.

Meet the Author

Dr. Leland Benton is Director of Applied Web Info, a holding company for ePubWealth.com, a leading ePublisher company based in Utah. With over 21,000 resellers in over 22-countries, ePubWealth.com is a leader in ePublishing, book promotion, and ebook marketing.

As the creator and author of "The ePubWealth Program," Leland teaches up-and-coming authors the ins-and-outs of today's ePublishing world. He has assisted hundreds of authors make it big in the ePublishing world.

Leland also created a series of external book promotion programs and teaches authors how to promote their books using external marketing sources.

Leland is also the Managing Director of Applied Mind Sciences, the company's mind research unit and Chief Forensics Investigator for the company's ForensicsNation unit. He is active in privacy rights through the company's PrivacyNations unit and is an expert in survival planning and disaster relief through the company's SurvivalNations unit.

Leland resides in Southern Utah.

http://www.amazon.com/author/lelandbenton

Visit some of his websites
http://appliedmindsciences.com/
http://appliedwebinfo.com/
http://BoolbuilderPLUS.com
http://embarrassingproblemsfix.com/
http://www.epubwealth.com/
http://forensicsnation.com/
http://neternatives.com/
http://privacynations.com/

http://survivalnations.com/
http://thebentonkitchen.com
http://theolegions.org